LIFE IN THE CITY AND ON THE FARM

THE GREAT DEPRESSION

EDITION

HISTORY 4TH GRADE

Children's History

Speedy Publishing LLC
40 E. Main St. #1156
Newark, DE 19711
www.speedypublishing.com

During the Great Depression life was difficult whether you were in the city or on the farm. In this book, you will learn about how people dealt with their troubles, whether they lived in the city or on the farm.

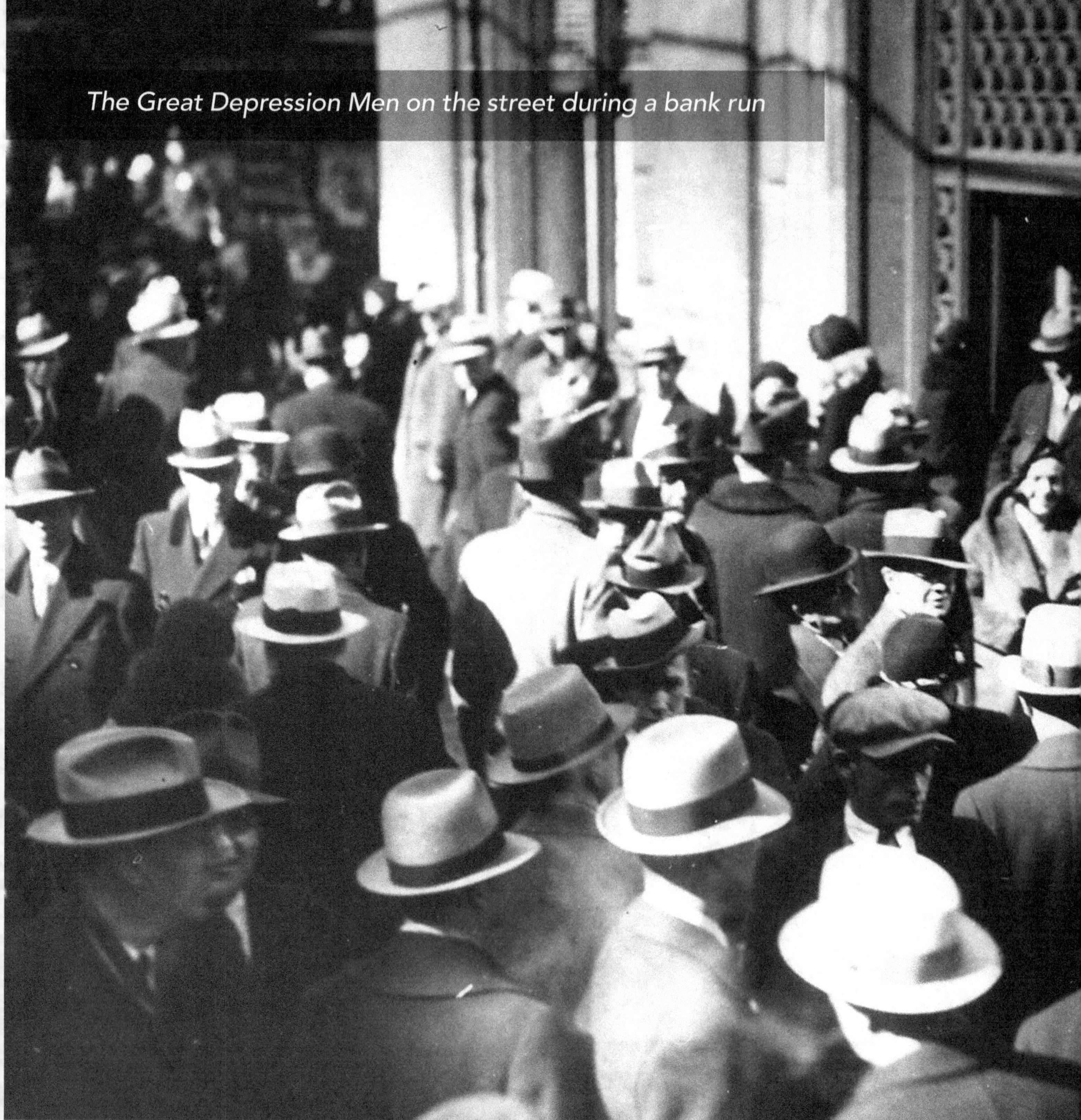
The Great Depression Men on the street during a bank run

SAFE
DEPOSIT

THE GREAT DEPRESSION

During the 1930s, there was a time of critical economic crisis known as the Great Depression. While it started in the United States, it spread quickly throughout most of the world. Many people were out of work, homeless and hungry during this time period. People stood in line at soup kitchens in the city just to get something to eat. Farmers in the country fought dust storms in the Midwest where a drought turned soil to dust.

It all started with the stock market crash in October 1929. Economists and historians state different causes for the depression that included overproduction of goods, consumer debt, drought, stock speculation and bank failures.

Police control a crowd of panicked depositors outside the Bowery Savings Bank of New York City in 1933.

On average, the family income dropped 40% during the Depression. Many people lost their savings because approximately 11,000 banks failed and over $1 billion in deposits were lost.

Unemployment was about 3% in 1929. It rose to 25% in 1933, and 1 out of 4 people were unemployed.

Men wait in line for food on East 25th Street New York City 1930.

Daily Life in the City

City life became quite difficult for most people. Jobs were hard to come by and food was scarce. Once someone would lose their job, they often would be evicted from their apartment or home.

They might be able to go live with a relative, or they might end up living in shack at a makeshift city known as a Hoovervilles. People that remained in their homes would often rent rooms to make money to pay the mortgage.

    Most families would take public transportation to the city instead of spending the money on gas and maintenance of a car.

    Some lost all their savings when their bank went out of business.

The Great Depression Unemployed men queued outside a soup kitchen opened in Chicago by Al Capone. The storefront sign reads 'Free Soup.

YED
HORA
BAILIFF
PARKING 25

WHAT'S FOR DINNER?

They typically did not have much to eat. They didn't have access to chickens, crops, or a vegetable garden like the farmers had. When the money was gone, they would have nothing to eat. They attempted many different ways to make what little bit of food they had last longer.

They created new recipes including *"Depression Cake"* which omitted difficult ingredients to obtain such as eggs and butter, and *"Mock Apple Pie"* which substituted crackers for apples. Many would eat dried beans, powdered milk, and potatoes.

A Hobo, Lou Ambers, tips his hat as he accepts a sandwich from a woman's hand during the Great Depression. Unemployed men were more reluctant than women to live with their relatives. 1935.

SOUP KITCHENS

To prevent people from going hungry, charities opened soup kitchens where people would be able to get a meal for free. People would sometimes wait for hours in line to maybe get some bread or a dish of watery soup. Soup was a popular meal since water could always be added to it to make more.

Bread line in Los Angeles serving soup and bread. The Spanish Colonial Church Neustra Senora La Reina de Los Angeles.

What Am I Going to Wear?

Purchasing new clothes was definitely not an option for most during this time period. People would either sew their own clothes or wear hand-me-downs from relatives.

Women would learn to sew in order to make sweaters and socks. They used cardboard for patching their shoes. They referred to it as **_"Hoover leather"_**, named for President Hoover.

I'M BORED!

People wanted to have fun in order to take their minds of their strife. They would enjoy going to the movies as well as listening to radio shows. The kids would play card games at home or stickball in the streets.

DO I HAVE TO GO TO SCHOOL?

Kids would still attend school during the Depression, but many would have to drop out once they turned 16 or 17 to get a job. Public schools often had to close or would not be able to afford the basic school necessities, such as books. Art, music, and sports programs were often cancelled in order to save money.

Hooverville at East 12th Street, New York City. Unemployed workers sit on crates by a shack with Christmas tree. January 1938 photo by Russell Lee.

KEEP
OUT

HOOVERVILLES

Most U.S. cities had areas where people that had been evicted from their homes would build small shack consisting of one room to live in. They were constructed from anything they were able to find including tar paper, cement blocks, cardboard, and wood scraps. These areas became known as **_"Hoovervilles"_**, named for President Hoover. These areas were often built close to soup kitchens where the residents could obtain a meal for free.

Great Depression Hooverville in Lower Manhattan. 1932.

WAS EVERYONE POOR?

No, not everyone was hungry, poor, or out of a job. Some had continued to work and had money for food and, sometimes, even for luxury items. Most people, however, had to cut back in order to make ends meet.

DAILY LIFE ON THE FARM

Life on a farm during the Depression was tough and a lot of hard work with very few luxuries. Most farmers had already been having a difficult time because of plunging prices and overproduction. In the Midwest, farmers had a particularly difficult time as years of drought and dust storms struck them during this time period.

WHAT'S FOR DINNER?

An advantage of living on a farm was that they could grow their food. They had milk, eggs, and vegetables which sometimes were difficult to get in the city. Occasionally, they would even have meat from pigs, cattle, or sheep.

I'M BORED!

Farm life entailed mostly hard work to just get by, but occasionally they would have some fun. They might get together for potluck dinners or dances. The kids would play games outside such as baseball and kick-the-can. In the evenings, families might listen to shows such as *Amos 'n' Andy* and *The Lone Ranger* on the radio.

DO I HAVE TO GO TO SCHOOL?

Some farm kids would attend school. In most of the rural areas, the school might be only a single room with one teacher teaching several grades. The kids often would have to walk a great distance to the school.

This would be quite dangerous during the dust storms and during the winter months. Even after being in school during the day, the children would still have hours of chores to complete once they arrived back at the farm.

Buried machinery in a barn lot in Dallas, South Dakota in 1936. The Dust Bowl ecological disaster extended from Texas into the Northern Plains and Canada.

What About the Dust Storms?

As the Midwest was struck with a drought during the Depression, the ground soil turned to dust. Farmers were not able to grow crops since there was not enough water. And making matters worse, dust storms started forming and covered everything with dust. It got everywhere, making life even more difficult.

CROPS

They often dealt with big grasshopper swarms that came out of nowhere and would eat all of their crops.

Sometimes they would burn their corn rather than wood for keeping their homes warm since they were not able to sell the corn, and the wood was too expensive to purchase.

In some of the areas, starving jackrabbits would come from the hills and devour and destroy their crops.

CALIFORNIA HERE WE COME!

Since the farmers were not able to produce crops due to the dust and the drought, they lost their farms. When they heard there was work available in California, thousands started the lengthy trip in hopes of finding work. Approximately 200,000 people made the move to California.

The great depression black and white photo from an old western ghost town in California.

WAS EVERYONE AFFECTED?

Even though it may not have been easy, some farmers survived. They were able to grow and sell enough crops and pay the mortgage so they could keep their farms. They were typically located in areas not affected by the dust storms and the drought.

Farmer stands in a dust storm in New Mexico, Spring 1935.

Franklin Delano Roosevelt Memorial Poor Farmers and Bread Line.

OUSED, ILL-CLAD, ILL-NOURISHED

HOW DID IT COME TO AN END?

The President when it began was Herbert Hoover and many citizens blamed him for it. Therefore, they named the small towns *"Hoovervilles"*. Franklin Roosevelt was elected in 1933 and promised the American people a *"New Deal"*.

The New Deal consisted of programs, laws, and government agencies that were enacted to assist in dealing with this awful time period. These laws put regulations on banks, the stock market and businesses.

North Dakota farmers waiting for their grants in a Resettlement Administration Office, precursor of the Farm Security Administration (FSA). July 1936 photo by Arthur Rothstein.

They also helped in putting people at work and tried helping to feed and house the poor. Several of these laws are still in force today, such as the Social Security Act.

It ended at the start of World War II. The economy of wartime put many back to work and factories were filled to capacity.

The Depression would leave a lasting legacy for the United States. The New Deal laws increased significantly government's role in people's daily lives. With construction of airports, parks, bridges, schools and roads, the public works department was able to enhance the infrastructure of the country.

The next time you think you have a terrible life, think about what life was like either in the city or on the farm during the Great Depression.

For additional information on life during the Great Depression, you can go to your local library, research the internet, and ask questions of your teachers, family and friends.

Visit
BABY PROFESSOR
EDUCATION KIDS
www.BabyProfessorBooks.com
to download Free Baby Professor eBooks
and view our catalog of new and exciting
Children's Books